5 FINGER
STAR WARS

Music by JOHN WILLIAMS

10 Exciting Selections from the Movie Saga
Arranged for Piano by Tom Gerou
With Optional Duet Accompaniments

T0055350

Foreword

10 of the most memorable pieces from the *Star Wars* films have been arranged in traditional five-finger style, with the melody split between the left and right hands, and without key signatures in the solo part. Starting hand positions are illustrated above each piece. Fingerings that are outside of the noted five-finger positions and those indicating a shift in hand position are circled ① for easy identification. Dotted quarter notes, triplets and sixteenth notes have been avoided. All of the melodic arrangements have optional duet accompaniments created to achieve a fuller, richer musical experience.

Contents

EXCLUSIVELY DISTRIBUTED BY

HAL•LEONARD®

Star Wars

("Main Theme") from *Star Wars*

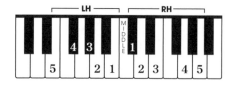

Music by **JOHN WILLIAMS**

Arr. by Tom Gerou

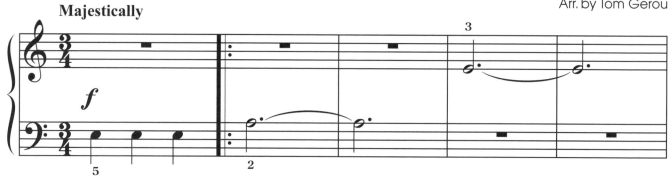

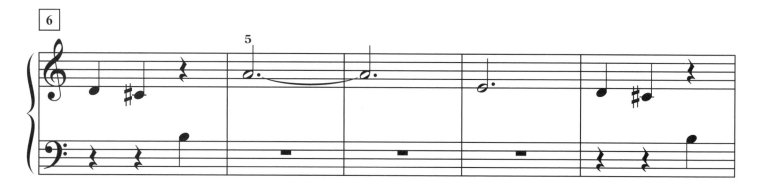

Optional Duet Accompaniment (Play solo part 1 octave higher than written.)

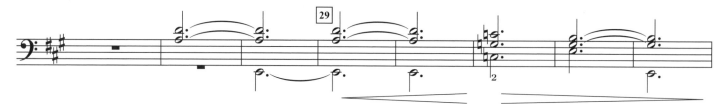

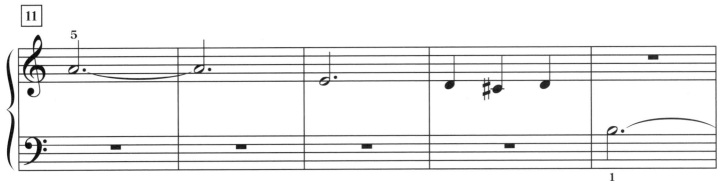

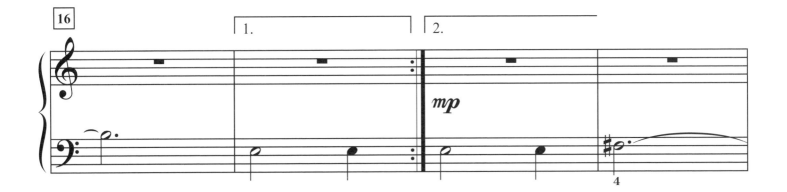

(duet continued)

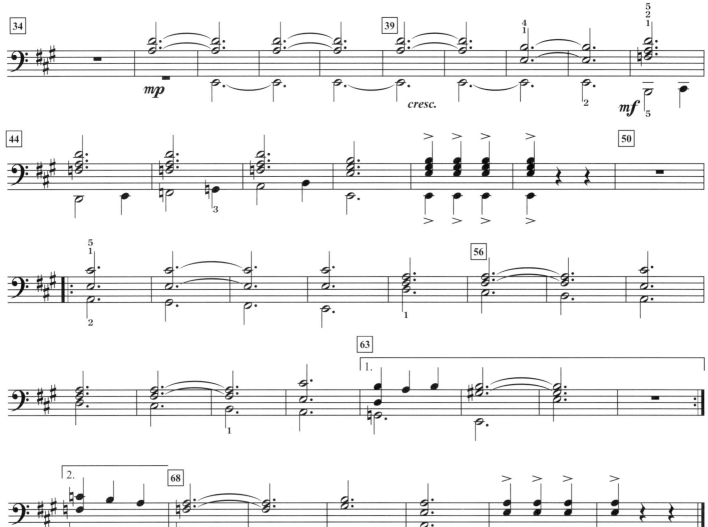

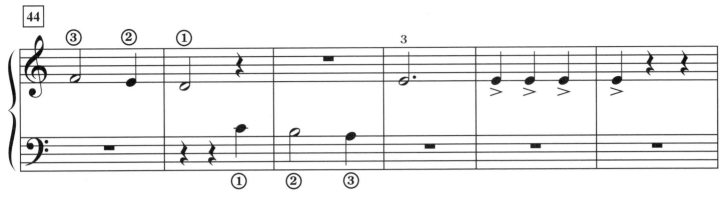

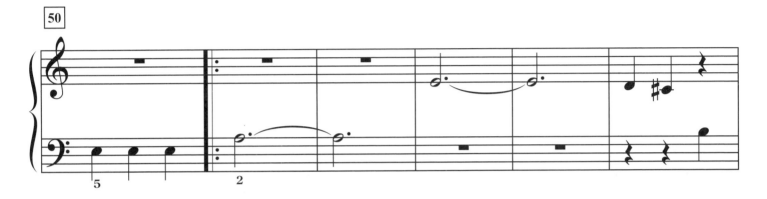

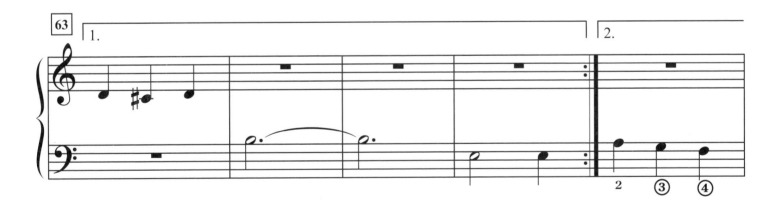

The Imperial March
("Darth Vader's Theme")
from *The Empire Strikes Back*

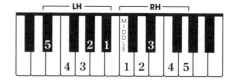

Music by **JOHN WILLIAMS**

Arr. by Tom Gerou

In march style

Optional Duet Accompaniment (Play solo part 1 octave higher than written.)

In march style

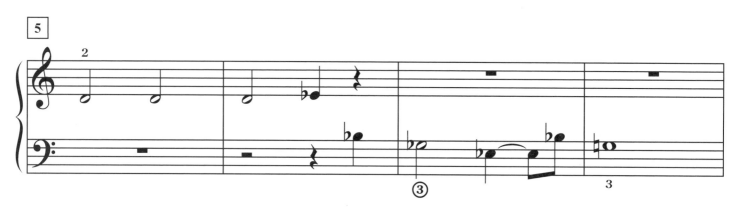

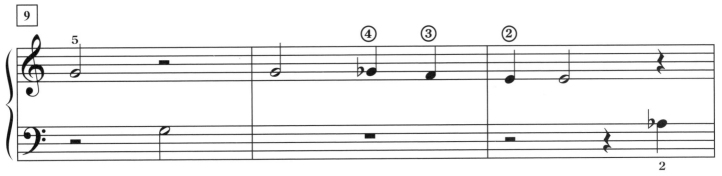

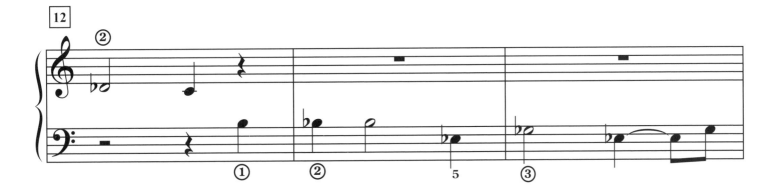

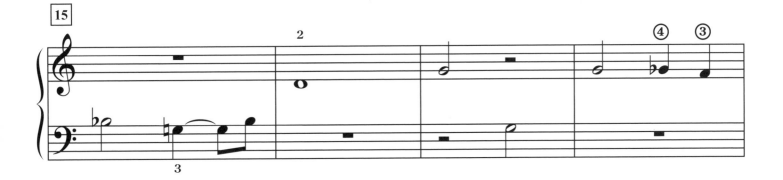

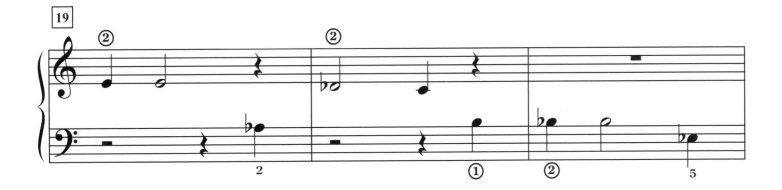

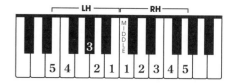

Luke and Leia
from *Return of the Jedi*

Music by **JOHN WILLIAMS**

Arr. by Tom Gerou

Optional Duet Accompaniment (Play solo part 1 octave higher than written.)

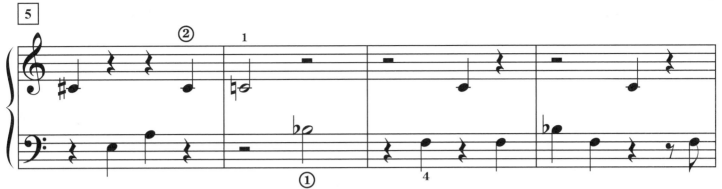

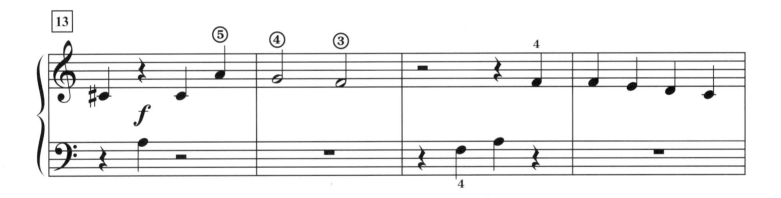

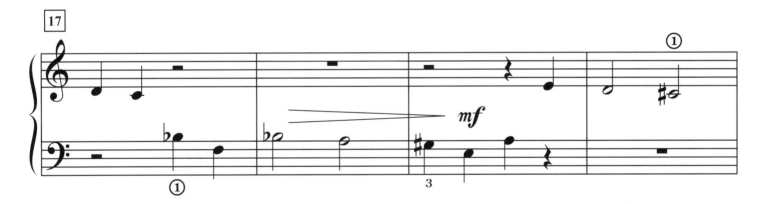

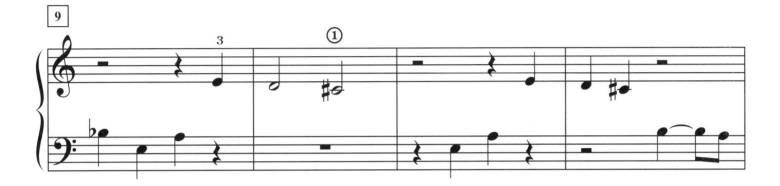

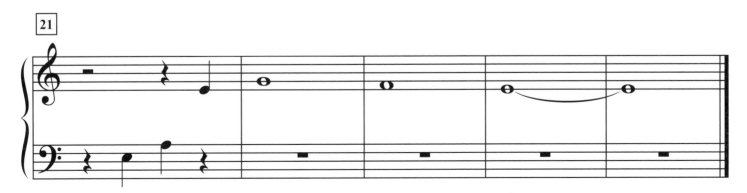

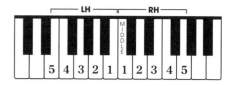

Across the Stars
("Love Theme")
from *Attack of the Clones*

Music by **JOHN WILLIAMS**

Arr. by Tom Gerou

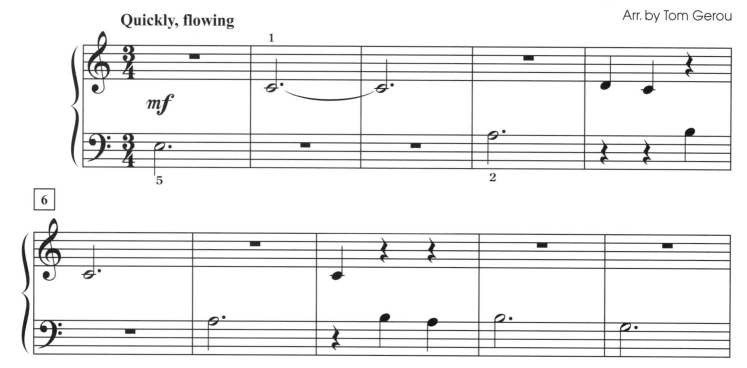

Optional Duet Accompaniment (Play solo part 1 octave higher than written.)

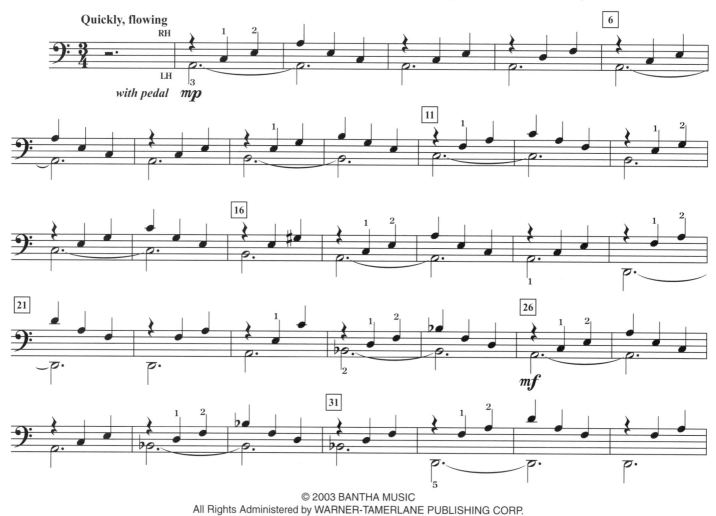

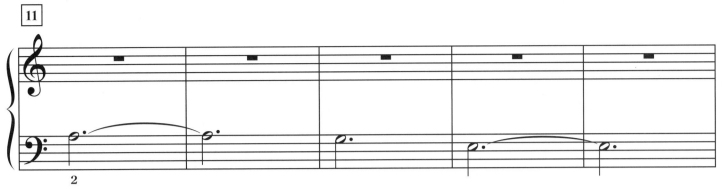

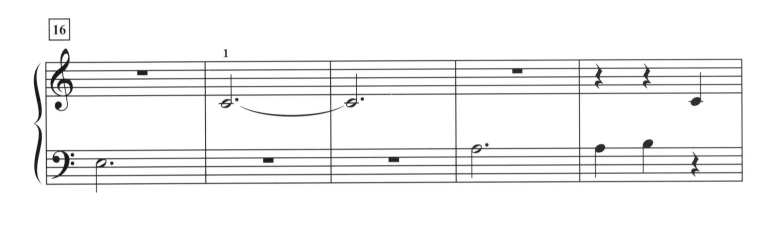

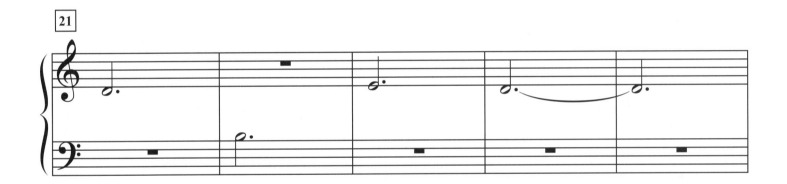

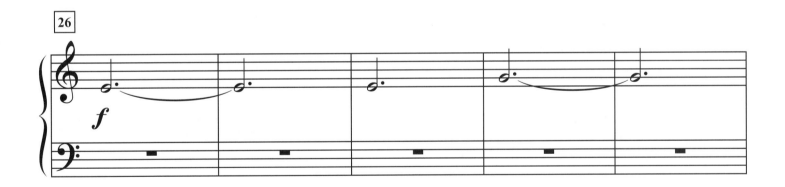

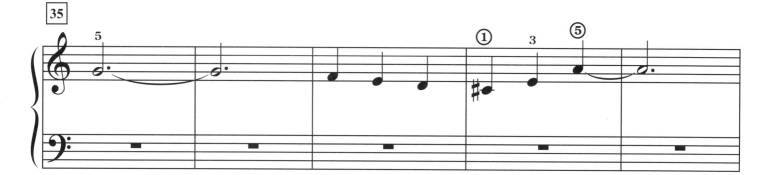

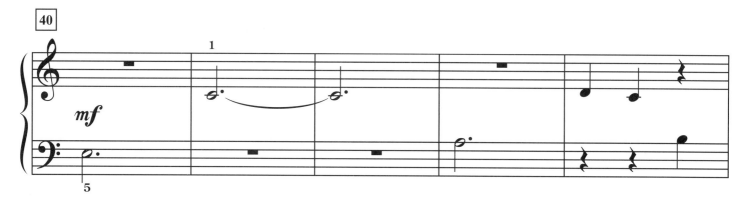

(duet continued)

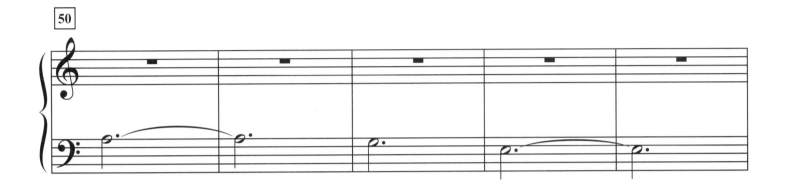

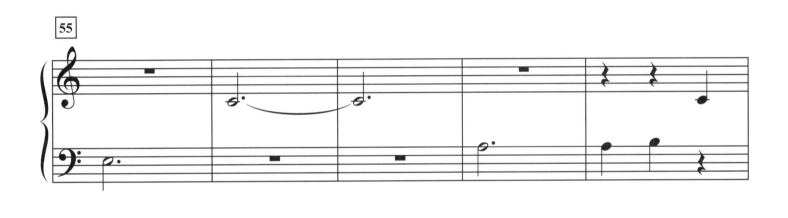

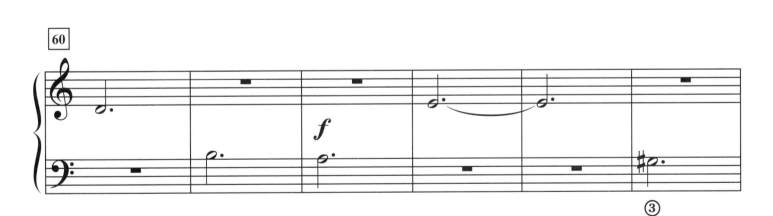

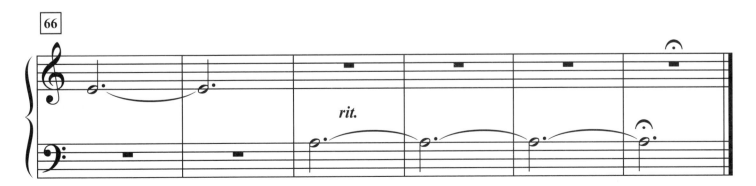

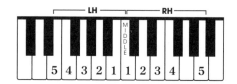

May the Force Be With You

("The Force Theme")

from *The Empire Strikes Back*

Music by **JOHN WILLIAMS**

Arr. by Tom Gerou

Optional Duet Accompaniment (Play solo part 1 octave higher than written.)

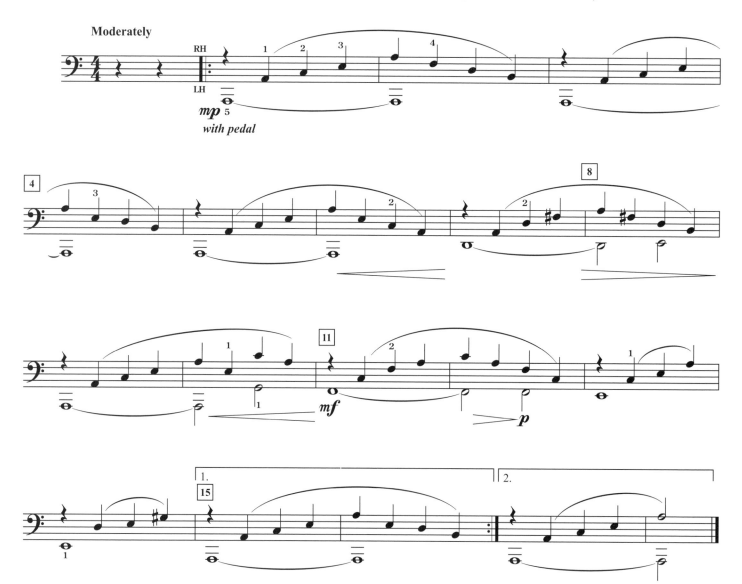

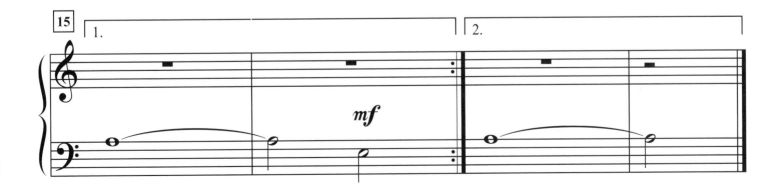

Princess Leia's Theme
from *Star Wars*

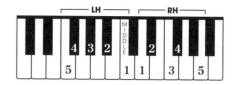

Music by **JOHN WILLIAMS**

Arr. by Tom Gerou

Optional Duet Accompaniment (Play solo part 1 octave higher than written.)

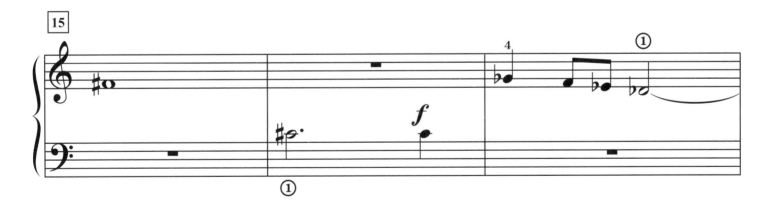

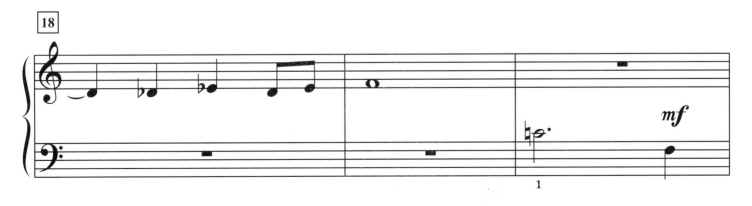

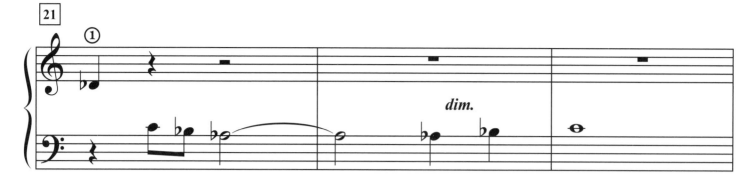

(duet continued)

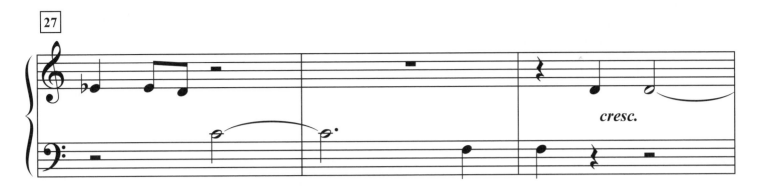

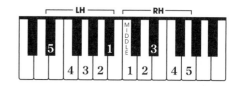

Yoda's Theme
from *The Empire Strikes Back*

Music by **JOHN WILLIAMS**

Arr. by Tom Gerou

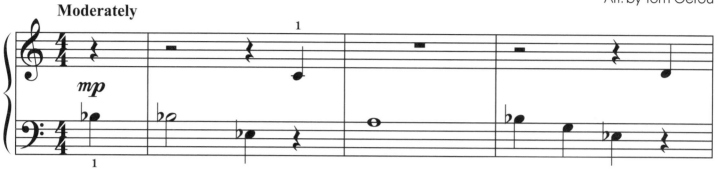

Optional Duet Accompaniment (Play solo part 1 octave higher than written.)

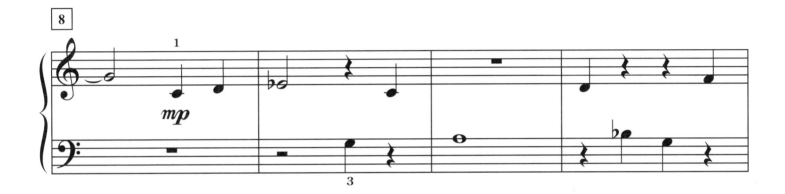

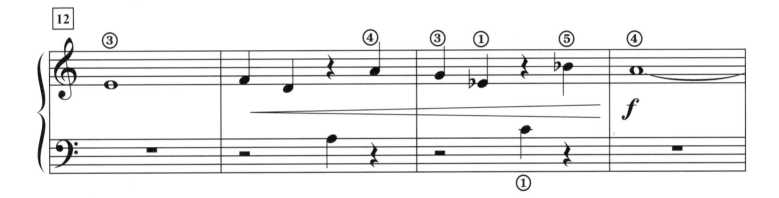

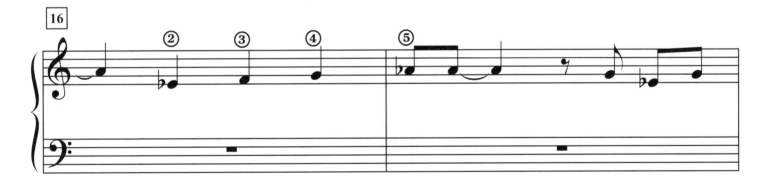

(duet continued)

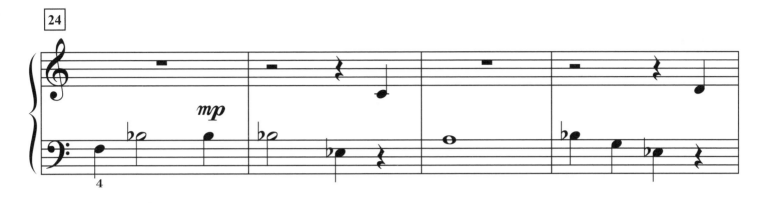

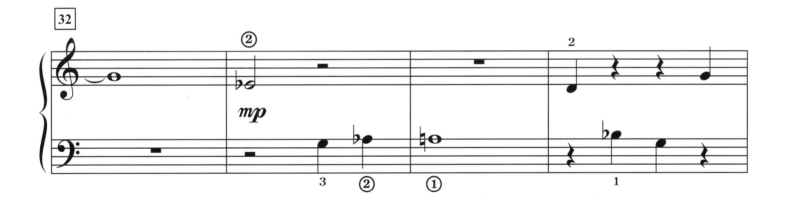

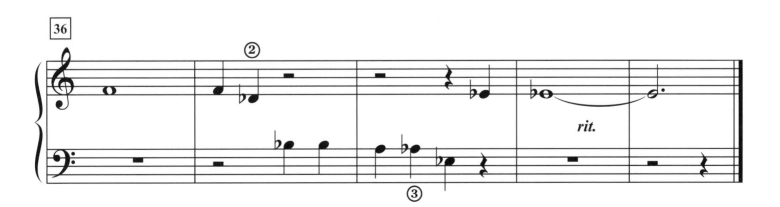

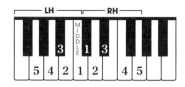

Cantina Band
from *Star Wars*

Music by **JOHN WILLIAMS**

Arr. by Tom Gerou

Optional Duet Accompaniment (Play solo part 1 octave higher than written.)

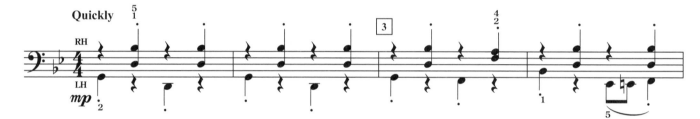

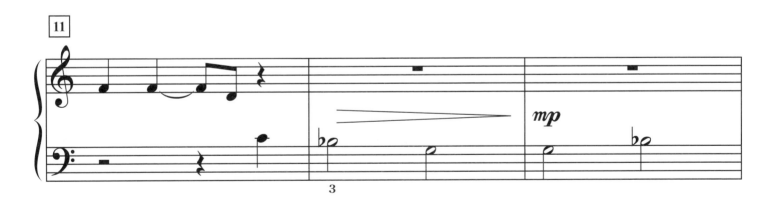

(duet continued)

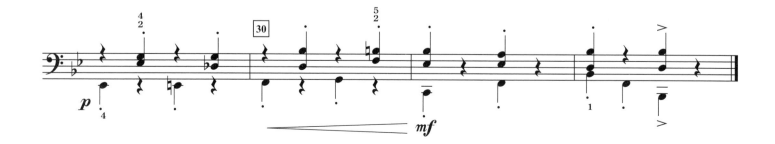

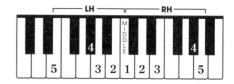

Duel of the Fates
from *The Phantom Menace*

Music by **JOHN WILLIAMS**

Arr. by Tom Gerou

Fast, with great force

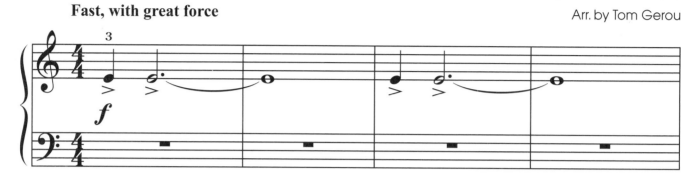

Optional Duet Accompaniment (Play solo part 1 octave higher than written.)

Fast, with great force

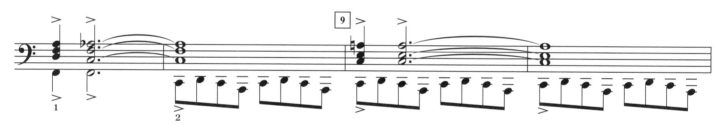

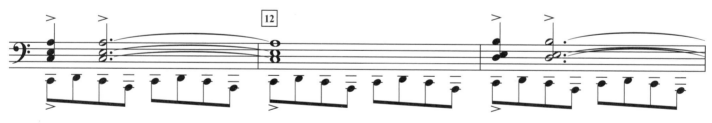

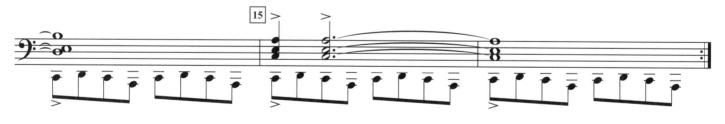

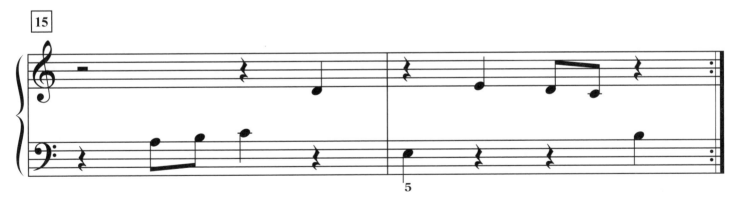

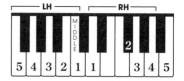

Anakin's Theme
from *The Phantom Menace*

Music by **JOHN WILLIAMS**

Arr. by Tom Gerou

Optional Duet Accompaniment (Play solo part 1 octave higher than written.)

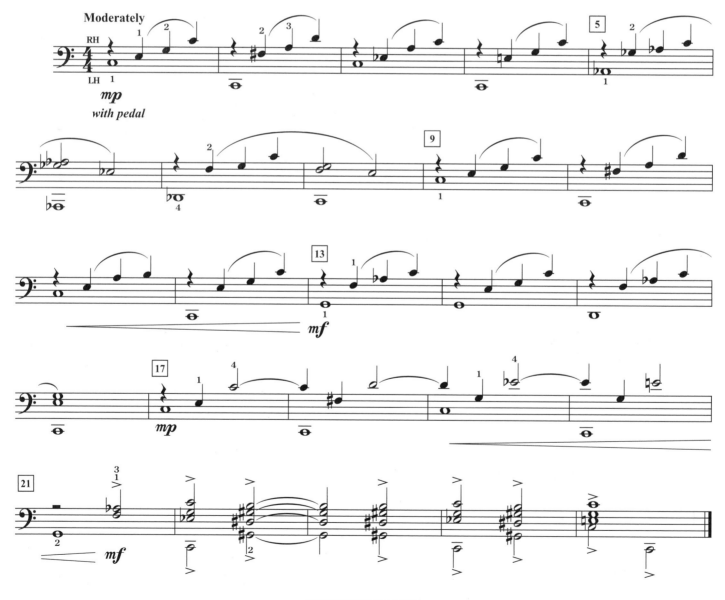

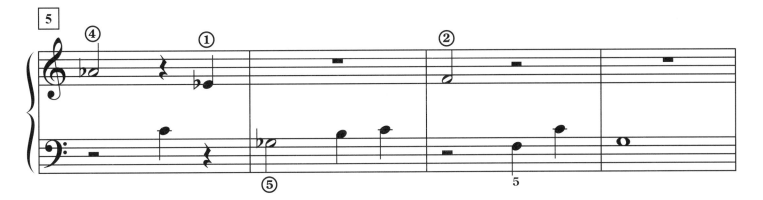

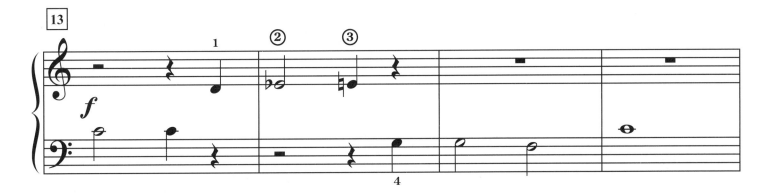

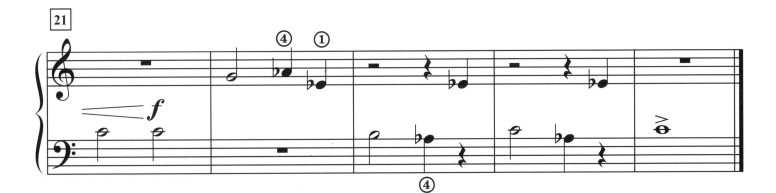